You Can Make a Difference!

Written by Mary-Anne Creasy

Flying Star
to Literacy

Contents

Introduction

Sometimes we find out about animals that need help. Sometimes we hear that the environment is in danger of being destroyed. These problems can seem too big to solve.

But some children have seen ways to help. These children are ordinary children just like you and they have made a difference.

Chapter 1

Saving
animals

My name is Alice.
When I was seven
years old, I went
on a holiday with
my family. I saw tigers
and lions in cages on
circus trucks.
The animals were sitting
in the hot sun without
water or shade.
I decided I wanted
to help animals like
them have better lives.

When I got home, I found out about a place that helps animals. This place looks after tigers and lions and other big cats that have not been looked after properly.

I decided to have a lemonade stand to raise money to help these big cats. I made posters and put them up in shop windows. The newspaper in my town saw the posters and did a story about what I was doing.

I raised nearly $800. I sent the money to the people who were looking after the big cats.

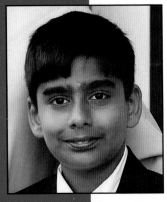

Chapter 2

Paper,
not plastic

My name is Abdul. When I was eight years old, I heard about how plastic bags are damaging the environment.

I decided to make bags out of old newspapers.

I took the bags to shops and got the owners to use them instead of plastic bags.

I have now made over 6000 paper bags, which I have given to shops in my town.

Some schools heard about what I was doing. They asked me to come and show them how to make the bags.

Now thousands of children are making paper bags. They give them to people to help save the environment.

People have also asked me to give talks about recycling and reducing waste.

Chapter 3

Saving
sea otters

My name is Ta'Kaiya and I live near the sea. I enjoy learning about the sea and the animals that live there.

I did a project on sea otters. I learned that oil spills from oil tankers kill sea otters and destroy their habitat. I wanted everyone to know about the problems caused by oil spills.

With help from my music teacher, I wrote a song about oil spills and how they damage the sea. More than 100 000 people have seen me sing my song.

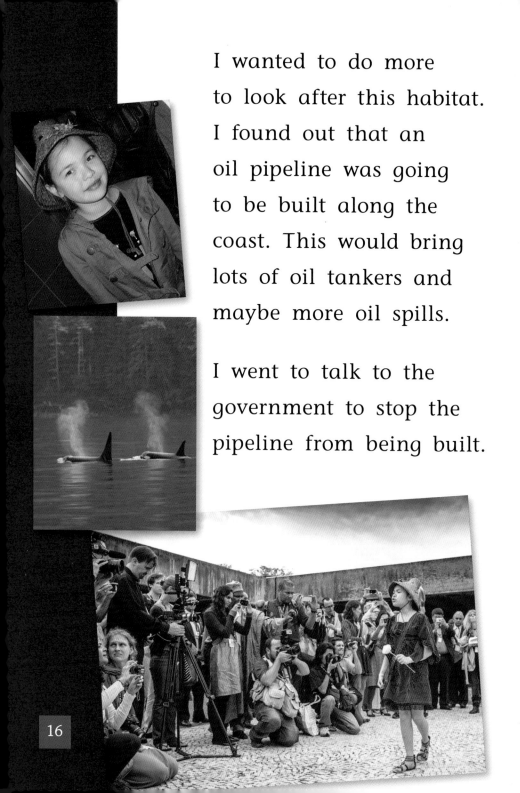

I wanted to do more to look after this habitat. I found out that an oil pipeline was going to be built along the coast. This would bring lots of oil tankers and maybe more oil spills.

I went to talk to the government to stop the pipeline from being built.

The government would not listen to me, but lots of people did. I now give talks to people about the environment.

Chapter 4

Saving South Yuba River State Park

This park is in California, USA. The government wanted to close this park, because it did not have the money to keep it open. This would mean that people could no longer visit the park.

The children at our school decided to try to stop the park from closing. This park was a place where we went to learn about nature and the environment.

We wrote speeches about why the park was important. We went on television and to the newspaper and talked about saving the park.

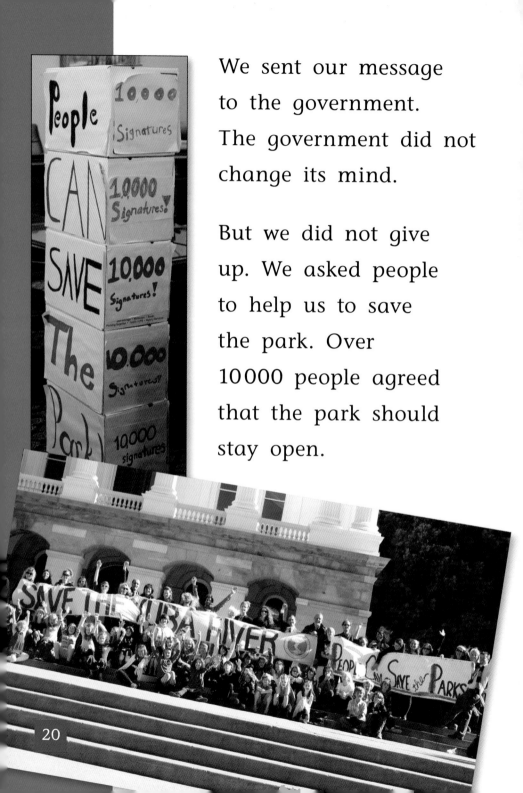

We sent our message to the government. The government did not change its mind.

But we did not give up. We asked people to help us to save the park. Over 10000 people agreed that the park should stay open.

We sent our message to
the government again.
This time it worked –
the government
found a way to
keep the park open.

Conclusion

This is what some of the children said about what they did.

> It doesn't matter what your age is. It just matters that you believe in something and that you're concerned and you're speaking out.

> I'm glad we saved this park, because all the next generations of my family will be able to see it.

Tigers are just like people – they need love and kindness too. Just because you're little doesn't mean you can't make a big difference. Saving tigers now means more tigers in the future.

I believe that if you have something good in your mind and convert it into action, you can save the world and serve the community.

A note from the author

When I read about some children who were taking action to solve environmental problems, I was amazed. They were challenging governments, solving pollution problems, and giving speeches around the world. These children were not afraid that they might fail. They just cared about their cause and believed in what they were doing.

I wanted to write about some of these children so that other kids could read about them and realise that they, too, can make a difference.